1

Table of Contents

CHAPTER ONE

How to care for orchids

Don't be intimidated by orchids if you're new to the hobby. There are a plethora of easy-to-grow orchids out there if you just take the time to learn about them. These aren't your typical houseplants in a pot. They're epiphytes, which means they grow on trees, not in the ground like most plants. Lady slippers are one of a few orchids that are semi-terrestrial and grow in the jungle's loamy soil.

"How do I care for orchids?" is a common question. Although orchid care is not difficult, it is just different from other types of plants. Even though they have a bad rep for being difficult to grow, orchids can actually thrive in a home environment thanks to a wide range of cultivars. A well-cared-for orchid can bloom for months at a time each year, and it can last a lifetime. Orchids, as far as flowering plants go, are a great deal. A well-maintained and diverse collection of orchids can provide year-round blooming. To properly care for orchids, all you need is a basic understanding of how orchids grow.

What you need to know to take good care of orchids

• The majority of orchids require weekly watering. Root rot can be caused by overwatering, so be careful not to overdo it.

Choose a sunny window sill that faces either east or west, and place your orchid on it.

• Feeding your orchids once a week with an orchid-specific fertilizer.

When your orchid stops blooming, you should repot it with new orchid mix.

There are numerous ways to take care of orchids.

As many as 880 genera and 22,000 species make up the

orchid family. Orchids are now the largest and most diverse group of flowering plants, and their numbers are increasing year after year. Most orchids are epiphytes, or "air plants," which cling to trees for support in tropical climates. Lithocytes, or "rock plants," are some types of orchids. Terrestrial orchids, which grow in the jungle's loamy detritus, make up the remainder. Providing general care instructions for orchids is difficult because the family is so diverse. A local nursery may have as few as a half-dozen of the few dozen commonly produced species. On our Orchid Identification page, you'll find an overview of many of the most common varieties. Hybrid plants are most likely to be found in retail locations such as nurseries, florists, hardware chains, and supermarkets. To achieve desirable traits like color, fragrance, flower size, and ease of care, orchid breeders have crossed different species and genera to create hybrids that combine the best of both worlds. If you take the time to learn about the basic requirements of today's orchid hybrids, growing them indoors can be a rewarding and easy experience.

The conditions in which orchids grow and how to take care of them

Imagine being in a jungle and looking up at a tree with an orchid clinging to it. As a result, the roots have clung to and are being supported by the tree. Only support and a small amount of food come from the organic matter decaying in the crook of the branches or from animal droppings that wash down in the rain. The orchid is not a parasite. The roots of these orchids are "epiphyte" because they are adapted to absorbing water from the humid air in the jungle. Many orchids have thick stems called "pseudobulbs" that allow them to store and hold water for the dry periods that will come because they have to deal with times of abundant water and times of dryness. Imagine this same plant in a typical home environment, in a pot of some sort. This must be a strange situation for the orchid, especially given how well it has adapted to its current environment. An understanding of the environment in which the orchid thrives is essential to its proper care. Our Orchid Starter Kits include everything you need to get your orchids off to a great start.

CHAPTER TWO

Frequently Asked Questions about Orchids

Understanding the orchid's needs for support, light, food, humidity, water, air movement, and temperature is critical to successful orchid care.

What is the best orchid mixture

In order to ensure healthy drainage and good airflow, the best orchid mixes include special medias. Orchids can't grow in dirt because their roots will be smothered and they'll die. Orchids grow best in specialized soil. That which is most appropriate to each type of orchid and its growing environment will be the ideal medium. Orchids can thrive in both a Florida sun porch and a heated Ohio home if they are cared for properly. Orchid mixes frequently contain a variety of media, each of which contributes a distinct set of desirable properties. Using an open, airy mix that provides the orchid with the proper amount of moisture is the goal in both cases.

We hope you'll see the wide variety of orchid media and mix ideas here, whether you choose one of our Classic Orchid Mixes, Imperial Orchid Mixes, or create your own custom Select-A-Blend. We've also included a diagram showing the relationship between orchid root size and mix choice. Please refer to our Media Weights chart to better understand the water retention capacity of each orchid media.

Orchid Knowledge

Orchids, in contrast to many other plants and animals, can produce hybrids between two different species or genera.

It is not uncommon for orchids to bloom more than once per year if they are kept in good condition.

• Orchids typically bloom for a period of six to ten weeks.

Many orchids are unable to flower for at least a year after being re-potted because of their sensitivity to re-potting.

When it comes to orchids, there are numerous varieties that share a number of characteristics, such as bilateral symmetry and extremely small seeds.

Easy Orchid Care Kits

The typical home poses some threats that Mother Nature does not, even though orchids have been around since the time of the T-Rex. Dry air and overwatering are the two most common causes of orchids' indoor failure. Using the supplies listed below, you can easily transform your house into a tropical haven for orchids. All of these items should be available at your neighborhood hardware store. Some of them may even be in your house already.

The following items are useful for taking care of orchids:

• A humidistat to monitor the level of moisture.

In order to maintain a high level of humidity, consider using a humidity tray.

• a fan for better air flow

In order to increase humidity, you can use a spritzer

For the sake of the orchid's health, you'll want to have a thermometer on hand.

Fertilizer for orchids that is specific to the time of year and the needs of your particular orchid

Maintaining the health of your orchids by using an orchid fungicide and bactericide

How to Take Care of Your Orchids

With the supplies in hand, we can now discuss how to care for the plants. When it comes to learning how to take care of orchids, there are a few things to keep in mind.

LIGHT

Orchids are extremely sensitive to light, especially when grown indoors. High light (unobstructed sunlight from a south-facing window) is preferred by some, while low light (no sunlight coming in through a window) is preferred by others (limited northern exposure).

Assess the leaves of your orchid if you are concerned about the amount of light it is receiving The presence of brown leaves on your plant is an indication that it requires less sunlight. Deep green leaves may need more light.

TEMPERATURE

Due to their tropical origins, many of the orchids sold as houseplants can be sensitive to sudden temperature changes. Keep an eye on the temperature and humidity levels your orchid prefers. Each of the most common orchids can be cared for in accordance with the detailed care guide below. Because your orchid is likely to be in the same condition if you're overheated or underheated.

Humidity

Tropical plants are used to a higher level of humidity than most people's homes. Place your potted orchid on top of pebbles and water it regularly to keep it healthy. In addition, air circulation is critical. If the condition of your orchid appears to be deteriorating, consider installing a fan in the room.

Orchids need watering.

Make sure the roots get a chance to soak up the water before it seeps into the soil. Simplify the process by placing your orchid in a sink and running room-temperature water over it. Don't use distilled or salt-softened water and give it time to drain completely.

It is important to water orchids in a different way than other plants because they are often planted in bark rather than soil. It's a good question, isn't it? Depending on the orchid species, pot, potting mix, humidity levels, and light conditions, watering may or may not be necessary at all.

When it comes to watering tolerant orchids like cattleyas, oncidiums, and dendrobiums, once a week is the rule of thumb. Every 4-5 days, water other species.

Orchid fertilization

Fertilizing, like other important aspects of care, is unique to each species. Weekly or monthly application of a fertilizer containing the ratio 20-20-20 is common practice among growers. For those who choose to fertilize weekly, it is essential that you dilute the fertilizer to avoid overfeeding the plant (about one-quarter of the full strength). You should continue to fertilize your plants even after the flowers have faded away.

TOXICITY

Generally speaking, orchids sold in stores are safe for humans and pets. Consumption, even if there are no long-term health consequences, is still discouraged. If you're keeping orchids indoors, make sure they're out of reach of curious children or pets.

some of the most common symptoms to look out for in the event of an accidental ingestion are:

- Headaches

- Nausea

- Vomiting

- Lethargy

CHAPTER THREE

Consult your doctor or a veterinarian if the symptoms persist. Identifying the species of your orchid will help you learn more about its potential dangers. Below you'll find a list of 23 commonly encountered species.

Problems caused by pests and pest control measures

Unfortunately, orchids are still vulnerable to pests and other health issues. Pest infestations can stunt new leaf growth, degrade stem health, and prevent flower growth, to name just a few of the problems they can cause. If you notice any of the following pests, then you should be on the lookout for them.

If you notice misshapen and discolored leaves on your orchid, it may have a pest problem. If your orchid isn't blooming or the flowers aren't maturing as expected, pests may be to blame. You may have a pest problem if your flowers are wilted or turning brown.

Propagation by means of REPOTTING

You want to keep your orchids growing and blooming so that you can enjoy them for many years to come. There are times when repotting is overlooked. Check out the frequently asked questions below for more information on repotting an orchid!

It's easy to share your orchid plant with loved ones once you've figured out how to make it rebloom. Make use of the plants you've grown from cuttings to decorate an area of your home that's been neglected.

It's an Orchid Checklist

Examine your orchid for signs of disease, weakening, or infestation in order to adjust your caregiving accordingly. Some species may not thrive in the environment you put them in, so be sure to ask an experienced and knowledgeable vendor for an orchid that will grow in the space you have available.

There are a number of indicators that your orchids are in need of attention, such as:

Crust and/or discoloration

• Webbing in white

Leaf wilting

Leaf color: yellow

• Spots that are brown or yellow

• Dark, moist areas

Tiny holes in the petals or leaves of wilted plants

COMMON QUESTIONS RELATED TO ORCHIDS

How do I care for orchids? What kind of supplies do I need? These are some of the most frequently asked questions about the plant.

INDOOR ORCHID PLANTS REQUIRE SPECIFIC MANAGEMENT.

The light requirements of various orchid species vary. Since not all rooms receive the same amount of light, finding the best location for your plant can be a challenge. When trying to figure out how to grow orchids indoors, a good rule of thumb is to look for a window that faces south or east. Avoid putting your orchid in direct sunlight at all costs.

WHAT HAPPENS TO ORCHIDS THAT FLOWER?

Orchids go into dormancy after their flowering period is over. Each species has a different life cycle, so the length of this period varies. Before they can start flowering again, the plants need to "rest." Reduce the amount of water you give your orchid after it has finished blooming.

Rot can kill plants of various species for a variety of reasons. Before watering your post-bloom orchid, make sure the soil is completely dry to the touch.

What are the best orchid pots?

Your orchid has a few choices when it comes to pots. If you're on a tight budget, a clear plastic pot is an excellent option. A clear plastic pot can mimic the natural exposure of orchid roots to sunlight found in the wild. To avoid overwatering, be sure to check for adequate drainage.

If you don't mind spending a little more money on a decorative touch, ceramic pots come in a wide range of designs and colors. Check for adequate drainage, just as you would with plastic pots. Look for small holes on the bottom of the container.

CHAPTER FOUR

The materials used to make woven mesh pots range widely. Using these containers closely mimics how orchids naturally grow is the biggest advantage. To prevent soil and roots from drying out too quickly, use a mesh pot if you live in a humid area.

ORCHIDS CAN BE REBORN

Flower shapes, sizes, and colors vary widely among orchids, making them instantly recognizable. If your orchid is waking up from its winter hibernation and you want to see it bloom once more, make sure you provide it with the best possible environment.

Maintain a temperature range of 55 to 65 degrees Fahrenheit when cooking in the pot. Use indirect lighting instead of direct sunlight when photographing. Before watering again, make sure the soil is completely dry, and keep track of when fertilizer may be needed. When a new flower spike appears, use a small stake and orchid clips to hold it in place.

A Beginner's Guide to Orchids

Although there are many beautiful orchid species, some are more fussy than others. Among the best orchids for novices are, but are not limited to, the following:

- Encyclia

- Brassavola

- Paphiopedilum

- Phalaenopsis

- Cattleya

The full species name can be found on all of the labels when purchasing your first orchid (ProFlowers offers a wide selection of orchids for delivery). If you can, inquire ahead of time to see if your local nursery carries the specific variety you're looking for. Check out the species-specific care guide below for more information on how to keep your plant in peak condition.

Care Requirements for the 23 Most Common Orchid Species

Species of orchids come in a wide range of care requirements. For the 23 most common species, we've compiled a list of the best ways to take care of them.

1. CYMBIDIUM

LIGHT

Filtering the light

SOIL

Mixture of peat moss or perlite and medium to fine fir bark

TEMPERATURE

As the seasons change, so do the temperature requirements of these orchids. Winter blooms are only triggered when temperatures drop to 45-55 degrees Fahrenheit. Leaves can burn if the temperature rises above 85 degrees.

WATER

Water in the morning to ensure that all of the moisture has been drained before the temperature begins to drop. Soggy soil can be avoided by allowing the soil to dry out slightly between waterings. The temperature affects how much water needs to be applied. Avoid over-watering your plants during winter and under-watering during summer.

FERTILIZER

Cymbidium orchids don't need a lot of extra nutrients. Add slow-release fertilizer pellets at the start of the season and you'll get good results. Make sure to use a well-balanced fertilizer, and only when your plants are in full bloom.

2. SARCOCHILUS

LIGHT

Low to moderate lighting

SOIL

Logs and river pebbles of a medium to coarse gradation

TEMPERATURE

For most sarcochilus to bloom, they require temperatures of at least 40 degrees Fahrenheit. They can withstand a light frost if they are protected from the elements and kept constantly circulating air.

WATER

The roots of the plant should be kept constantly moist in the potting soil. During the winter, be especially careful not to overwater your plants.

CHAPTER FIVE

FERTILIZER

When a child's growth is active,
it's best to feed them lightly.
This is the perfect time to use a
well-balanced   water-soluble
fertilizer.

3. PHALAENOPSIS

LIGHT

Indirect light that is medium to
bright.

SOIL

orchid bark or orchid mix, either of which is a good well-draining potting medium.

TEMPERATURE

The daytime temperature ranges from 68 to 85 degrees Fahrenheit. When in bloom, the temperature needs to be maintained at a constant level, even at night. Flowers and buds can be damaged by cold or drafty conditions.

WATER

Allow the potting mix to almost completely dry between waterings, and water only once per week. Keep it out of the water.

FERTILIZER

When the orchid is not in bloom, apply phalaenopsis fertilizer at one-quarter strength every other watering. Flowering can be boosted by using fertilizer.

4. DENDROBIUM

LIGHT

Morning sun and afternoon shade

SOIL

orchid bark or orchid mix, either of which is a good well-draining potting medium.

TEMPERATURE

The daytime temperature ranges from 68 to 85 degrees Fahrenheit. When in bloom, the temperature needs to be maintained at a constant level, even at night. Flowers and buds can be damaged by cold or drafty conditions.

WATER

Allow the potting soil to almost dry out between waterings by watering once a week. Keep it out of the water.

FERTILIZER

Fertilizer isn't necessary when your orchid is in bloom. Every other watering in the summer should include a balanced fertilizer. In the fall, stop fertilizing. Consider using a high-phosphorus fertilizer in January if there is no new growth.

5. CATTLEYA

LIGHT

Morning sun and afternoon shade

SOIL

Medium-grade fir bark, for example

TEMPERATURE

Temperatures below 85 degrees Fahrenheit are ideal for them during the day. They prefer slightly cooler temperatures at night. Temperature extremes can be tolerated if they are short-lived and not repeated.

WATER

Water plants only when the potting soil is dry, not when it's wet. These plants are accustomed to drying out between rains because they grow in the treetops.

FERTILIZER

At 1 teaspoon per gallon of water, high-nitrogen fertilizers can be used all year long and are safe to use. Once a month, give your pet a meal.

6. VANDA

LIGHT

Morning sun and afternoon shade

SOIL

Medium-grade fir bark, for example

TEMPERATURE

The daytime temperature should be no more than 85 degrees Fahrenheit for them to thrive. They prefer slightly cooler temperatures at night. Temperature extremes can be tolerated if they are short-lived and not repeated.

CHAPTER SIX

WATER

When it rains, these plants tend to dry out in the treetops, where they can be exposed to the elements for long periods. Wait until the potting medium has dried out completely before watering it again.

FERTILIZER

All year round, high-nitrogen fertilizers can be used. Fertilize your plants once a month with a solution of 1 teaspoon and 1 gallon of water.

7. PAPHIOPEDILUM

LIGHT

Low-level illumination

SOIL

Mixture of peat moss or perlite and medium to fine fir bark

TEMPERATURE

Maintaining a temperature range of 60-80 degrees Fahrenheit is recommended for plants with mottled leaves. Paphiopedilums with mottled leaves, which are more common, can withstand temperatures as low as 50 degrees F on a regular basis.

WATER

Five days of watering. Keep an eye on the top to see if it's dry, and don't overwater.

FERTILIZER

This type of plant requires very little fertilization. Use a high-nitrogen fertilizer during the growing season if the plant is in bark. It's best to use a balanced fertilizer once a month in a half-strength form and flush it out with clear water every other week.

8. ONCIDIUM

LIGHT

Morning sun and afternoon shade

SOIL

Fine-grade bark or orchid mix can be used as a potting medium.

TEMPERATURE

Temperatures ranging from 55 to 85 degrees Fahrenheit are suitable for these orchids. If there is enough air movement, Oncidiums can withstand higher temperatures.

WATER

This plant does not adhere to a regular watering routine. Popsicle sticks can be used to test for moisture in the potting mix. A plant's watering requirements can fluctuate from daily to weekly as the growing season progresses.

FERTILIZER

During the growing season, apply a high-nitrogen fertilizer to the bark of the orchid. Otherwise, fertilize every other week with a balanced fertilizer diluted to half strength and flush the fertilizer once a month with clear water. When the weather is sunny, apply more fertilizer.

9. MILTONIA

LIGHT

With a soft diffused glow

SOIL

Fine-grade bark or orchid mix can be used as a potting medium.

TEMPERATURE

Temperatures below 85 degrees Fahrenheit are ideal for them

during the day. During the night, they are able to tolerate slightly lower temperatures. Temperature extremes can be tolerated if they are short-lived and not repeated.

WATER

Miltonias require more frequent watering because they grow all year long. Once a week in the winter and twice a week in the summer are typical watering schedules for these plants.

FERTILIZER

At 1 teaspoon per gallon of water, high-nitrogen fertilizers can be used all year long and are safe to use. Once a month, fertilize.

10. ODONTOGLOSSUM

LIGHT

Low light is filtered out

CHAPTER SEVEN

SOIL

Fine-grade bark or orchid mix can be used as a potting medium.

TEMPERATURE

Temperatures between 75 and 85 degrees Fahrenheit are ideal for them during the day. During the night, they are able to tolerate slightly lower temperatures.

WATER

Avoid over-watering the plant. Drink more water when plants are growing.

FERTILIZER

At least once a month, apply orchid fertilizer to your plants.

11. VUYLSTEKEARA

LIGHT

Low light is filtered out

SOIL

Fir bark that is medium to fine in texture.

TEMPERATURE

Temperatures between 75 and 85 degrees Fahrenheit are ideal for them during the day. During the night, they are able to tolerate slightly lower temperatures.

WATER

Avoid over-watering the plant. Drink more water when plants are growing.

FERTILIZER

At least once a month, apply orchid fertilizer to your plants.

12. ZYGOPETALUM

LIGHT

Midday shade in the morning and afternoon sun

SOIL

Fine-grade bark or orchid mix can be used as a potting medium.

TEMPERATURE

As long as the plant is climatized, Zygopetalum orchids can thrive in both hot summers and cold winters. Temperatures below 35 degrees Fahrenheit should be avoided as soon as the plant's spikes or flowers appear. Avoid frost with these plants at all costs.

WATER

Watering the plant every 7-10 days is recommended. Don't allow the bark to dry out to the point of sogginess, but also don't allow it to dry out completely.

FERTILIZER

From spring to summer, use high-nitrogen fertilizers, and from fall to winter, use low-nitrogen fertilizers. Fertilize once a month by mixing 1 teaspoon of fertilizer with 1 gallon of water.

13. LUDISIA

LIGHT

The glow of soft, diffused light.

SOIL

Mixture of 60% potting soil and 40% grit or perlite or sand

TEMPERATURE

Temperature tolerance for these orchids is a wide range of 55-85 degrees Fahrenheit. Make sure they are never exposed to temperatures lower than 50 degrees.

WATER

Slightly wet conditions are ideal for this plant. Do not allow it to dry out between waterings.

FERTILIZER

The orchid Ludisia is a small feeder. Fertilizer is only needed a few times per year. A special orchid feed or a more general fertilizer can be used.

14. PHAIUS

LIGHT

With a soft diffused glow

SOIL

Potting soil for indoor plants that drains well

TEMPERATURE

Temperatures between 75 and 85 degrees Fahrenheit are ideal for them during the day. During the night, they are able to tolerate slightly lower temperatures.

WATER

Slightly wet conditions are ideal for this plant. Do not allow it to dry out between waterings.

FERTILIZER

Fertilize every other watering when the weather is warm or if you live in a warm climate.

15. PHRAGMIPEDIUM

LIGHT

With a soft diffused glow

SOIL

For drainage, consider using tree fern in addition to seedling-grade fir bark mixes.

TEMPERATURE

Temperatures between 75 and 85 degrees Fahrenheit are ideal for them during the day. During the night, they are able to tolerate slightly lower temperatures. Good air circulation is essential.

WATER

These plants are best grown in saucers filled with half an inch of fresh water because they prefer moist conditions. The water should be refilled as soon as it is nearly gone.

FERTILIZER

Every other watering, apply a low-nitrogen fertilizer to the soil. Rinsing the pots and saucers, especially if they are made of clay, is essential to remove accumulated fertilizer.

16. BRASSAVOLA

LIGHT

With a soft diffused glow

SOIL

Fine-grade orchid bark or orchid mix, preferably with clay pellets, charcoal, and pine bark chips in the potting medium is ideal.

TEMPERATURE

Brassavolas prefer temperatures in the mid- to upper-elevation range. Temperatures between 65 and 85 degrees are ideal for the plants to thrive and produce flowers.

WATER

During the growing season, water frequently, but allow the soil to dry out slightly after the flowers have faded.

FERTILIZER

A weak fertilizer solution should be used year-round to feed the orchid.

17. CYCNOCHES

LIGHT

Diffused light with a warm glow

SOIL

Fine-grade bark or orchid mix can be used as a potting medium.

CHAPTER EIGHT

TEMPERATURE

At night, the ideal temperature ranges from 60-65 degrees Fahrenheit to 75-80 degrees. Temperature extremes can be tolerated if they are short-lived and not repeated. Maintaining a reasonable temperature will ensure that your plant is healthy.

WATER

Cycnoches require more frequent watering because they grow all year long. Once a week in the winter and twice a week in the summer are the typical watering schedules for these plants.

FERTILIZER

Fertilizers high in nitrogen can be used all year round. Fertilize once a month by mixing 1 teaspoon of fertilizer with 1 gallon of water.

18. CATASETUM

LIGHT

a dazzling source of illumination

SOIL

Smaller pots use fine-grade orchid bark, while larger pots use medium-grade bark.

TEMPERATURE

These orchids prefer temperatures ranging from 80 to 100 degrees Fahrenheit during the day and 60 to 65 degrees at night, which is typical of their native tropical habitat. Temperatures should fall to 70-

85 degrees during the day and 55 degrees at night when the growing season is over.

WATER

The lifespan of these plants is short. When new leaves begin to emerge, begin watering once a week. When growth halts, gradually decrease watering.

FERTILIZER

Use a high-nitrogen formulation while plants are actively growing, then reduce nitrogen use gradually as the growth period concludes... Only plants that normally bloom in the spring should use bloom booster fertilizer in the fall.

19. EPIDENDRUM

LIGHT

Indirect light that is medium to bright.

SOIL

Fine-grade bark or orchid mix can be used as a potting medium.

TEMPERATURE

Temperatures should be between 60 and 90 degrees Fahrenheit during the day and between 50 and 70 degrees at night. For brief periods, these orchids can withstand temperatures as low as near-freezing.

WATER

More frequent and more generous watering is required for Epidendrum orchids. During the warmer months, water every 4-5 days, and once a week in the cooler months.

FERTILIZER

The best time to fertilize is when a plant is in full bloom. Every time you water, use a half-strength solution of a balanced fertilizer.

20. ENCYCLIA

CHAPTER NINE

LIGHT

a dazzling source of illumination

SOIL

Coarse fir bark potting mix that quickly drains

TEMPERATURE

The ideal temperature range for this plant is 70 degrees Fahrenheit during the day and 55-60 degrees Fahrenheit at night.

WATER

These plants prefer a dry environment. Increase watering slightly when growth begins during the winter months.

FERTILIZER

Fertilize encyclia orchids once a week while they are actively growing. An orchid fertilizer mix should be used. Encyclias should only be fertilized once a month during the winter months.

21. LYCASTE

LIGHT

Filtered sunlight with a bright radiance.

SOIL

Potting soil made from fine fir bark and sphagnum moss

TEMPERATURE

Temperatures between 75 and 85 degrees Fahrenheit are ideal for them during the day. During the night, temperatures between 50 and 60 degrees are ideal.

WATER

At this point, water the plant's potting mix until it's almost dry to the core. When watering, be sure to thoroughly soak the potting mix. In the summer, this can happen every two to three days, and in the winter, it can happen every seven to ten days.

FERTILIZER

During the growing season, these plants should receive a

monthly dose of a water-soluble, balanced fertilizer.

22. MASDEVALLIA

LIGHT

The light level is between medium and low.

SOIL

Potting soil made from fine fir bark and sphagnum moss

TEMPERATURE

Temperatures between 75 and 85 degrees Fahrenheit are ideal for them during the day. They prefer nighttime temperatures of between 50 and 60 degrees Fahrenheit.

WATER

This plant prefers a slightly moist but not wet environment. When watering, be sure to thoroughly soak the potting mix. Every 2-3 days in the summer and every 7-10 days in the winter is an appropriate amount of water to use.

FERTILIZER

Every third watering, use a small amount of half-strength fertilizer.

23. PSYCHOPSIS

LIGHT

Light levels range from dim to bright.

SOIL

Fine-grade orchid bark or orchid mix, preferably with clay pellets, charcoal, and pine bark chips in the potting medium is ideal.

TEMPERATURE

Temperatures between 75 and 85 degrees Fahrenheit are ideal for them during the day. During the night, temperatures between 50 and 60 degrees are ideal.

WATER

During the summer, these plants need to be watered every

two or three days. Cooler climates allow for less frequent watering.

FERTILIZER

Grow periods and brighter light conditions are the best times to apply fertilizer. It is possible to use any type of orchid-friendly fertilizer, but a fir bark mix will require less nitrogen.

To become an orchid expert, you'll need to follow all of these tips. Make sure you tell your loved ones how to properly care for your orchids before you give them a beautiful and meaningful gift!

THE END